UNLOCKING SUCCESS

Proven Strategies to Build Wealth, Achieve Freedom, and Thrive in 2025

CONSULTORIA IA

Copyright © 2024 CONSULTORIA IA

All rights reserved

The characters and events portrayed in this book are fictitious. Any similarity to real persons, living or dead, is coincidental and not intended by the author.

No part of this book may be reproduced, or stored in a retrieval system, or transmitted in any form or by any means, electronic, mechanical, photocopying, recording, or otherwise, without express written permission of the publisher.

Cover design by: Art Painter
Library of Congress Control Number: 2018675309
Printed in the United States of America

TO OUR FAMILY

CONTENTS

Title Page
Copyright
Dedication
Brief Oveview
Target Audience
Why read this book
Preface
Chapter 1: The Mindset of Success: Shifting Perspectives for Growth and Wealth
Chapter 2: Building Wealth: Strategies to Multiply Your Income Streams
Chapter 3: Freedom through Financial Independence: Mastering Your Money
Chapter 4: Thriving in 2025: Embracing Change and Capitalizing on Trends
Chapter 5: From Vision to Reality: Creating and Executing Your Master Plan
Appendices

BRIEF OVEVIEW

Unlocking Success: Proven Strategies to Build Wealth, Achieve Freedom, and Thri in 2025 is a comprehensive guide to navigating the challenges and opportunities modern life. This ebook offers actionable insights into building sustainable weal achieving personal and financial freedom, and thriving in a rapidly evolving world.

Packed with proven strategies, real-world case studies, and inspiring examples, the bo empowers readers to unlock their full potential. Whether you're an entrepreneur, professional, or someone seeking financial independence, **Unlocking Success** provides t tools and mindset to succeed in 2025 and beyond.

TARGET AUDIENCE

The target audience for **Unlocking Success: Proven Strategies to Build Wealth, Achieve Freedom, and Thrive in 2025** includes:

1. **Entrepreneurs and Business Owners**
   - Individuals seeking practical strategies to grow their businesses, increase profits, and adapt to market trends in 2025.
2. **Professionals and Aspiring Leaders**
   - Those aiming to advance their careers, achieve financial freedom, and develop leadership skills in a competitive environment.
3. **Young Adults and Millennials**
   - Individuals eager to start their journey toward wealth building and personal development while leveraging modern opportunities.
4. **Investors and Financial Planners**
   - People looking for insights into managing finances effectively and creating sustainable wealth in an evolving economy.
5. **Self-Improvement Enthusiasts**
   - Readers who value personal growth, time management, and strategies for achieving a balanced, thriving life.
6. **Digital Nomads and Freelancers**
   - Individuals seeking freedom through flexible work arrangements and exploring opportunities in the digital age.
7. **Anyone Facing Change in 2025**
   - Those looking to navigate uncertainty, embrace innovation, and thrive in a world of rapid transformation.

WHY READ THIS BOOK

Here's why **Unlocking Success: Proven Strategies to Build Wealth, Achieve Freedom and Thrive in 2025** is a must-read:

1. **Actionable Strategies**
   - The book delivers practical, step-by-step strategies to help you build wealth, achieve financial freedom, and thrive in a rapidly changing world.
2. **Future-Focused Insights**
   - It's tailored to the challenges and opportunities of 2025, offering relevant advice on navigating economic shifts, technological advancements, and evolving markets.
3. **Comprehensive Approach**
   - From mindset transformation to financial planning and career growth, the book covers every aspect of achieving success and balance in life.
4. **Real-World Examples**
   - With inspiring case studies and examples, the book bridges the gap between theory and practical application, making success achievable for everyone.
5. **Time-Tested Wisdom**
   - Learn from proven strategies and timeless principles, reimagined for the realities of the modern world.
6. **Empowerment and Motivation**
   - It inspires readers to take charge of their future, overcome challenges, and unlock their full potential.
7. **Tailored for a Broad Audience**
   - Whether you're an entrepreneur, professional, or someone seeking self improvement, the book speaks to diverse needs and aspirations.

Reading this book equips you with the mindset, tools, and strategies to thrive in 2025 and beyond. It's not just a guide—it's a blueprint for lasting success.

PREFACE

The world in 2025 is brimming with opportunities, yet it's also a time of rapid change, uncertainty, and challenges. Success today requires more than just hard work; it demands strategy, adaptability, and a clear vision of what you want to achieve.

Unlocking Success: Proven Strategies to Build Wealth, Achieve Freedom, and Thrive in 2025 was born from a deep desire to empower individuals to take control of their lives and thrive in this dynamic era. Over the years, I've witnessed countless stories of triumph and failure—stories that reveal patterns, principles, and strategies that separate those who merely survive from those who truly thrive.

In this book, I've distilled these insights into practical, actionable steps that anyone can follow. Whether you're an entrepreneur striving to grow your business, a professional seeking financial freedom, or simply someone eager to create a fulfilling and prosperous life, this book is for you.

The journey to success is personal, but the principles are universal. This book blends timeless wisdom with modern innovation, offering you tools and perspectives to unlock your potential and achieve the life you've always dreamed of.

As you turn these pages, remember: success isn't just about wealth or achievements—it's about living a life of purpose, freedom, and joy. Let this book be your guide to unlocking the future you deserve.

Here's to your success in 2025 and beyond.

CONSULTORIA IA

CHAPTER 1: THE MINDSET OF SUCCESS: SHIFTING PERSPECTIVES FOR GROWTH AND WEALTH

Success begins in the mind. It's a truth often repeated, yet seldom fully grasped. T： mindset you cultivate shapes your decisions, actions, and ultimately your life trajectory. For anyone aiming to build wealth, achieve freedom, and thrive in 202 adopting the right mental framework is not optional—it is essential. In this chapte we'll explore how to rewire your thoughts, embrace a growth-oriented perspectiv and internalize the habits and attitudes that lead to lasting success.

The Power of Belief: Seeing Possibilities, Not Limitations

One of the most significant barriers to success is a fixed mindset. This mental state se talent, intelligence, and circumstances as static, unchangeable factors that dictate yo future. If you believe you're not "good with money" or "not entrepreneurial," y unconsciously limit your potential. To succeed, you must shed this belief system and ado a growth mindset—a conviction that abilities can be developed and that challenges a opportunities for learning.

Dr. Carol Dweck, in her groundbreaking work on growth mindset, explains that individua who believe they can improve their skills are far more likely to achieve success. F instance, instead of avoiding financial planning because it feels overwhelming, approach as a skill you can master over time. Recognize that every expert was once a beginner, a every setback is a stepping stone toward mastery.

To start shifting your beliefs, take an inventory of your self-talk. Are your inner though filled with "I can't," "I'll never," or "I'm not capable"? Replace these with empoweri alternatives like "I'm learning," "I'll figure it out," and "This is a challenge I can overcom Visualization can also play a transformative role—imagine yourself succeeding in viv detail. See yourself thriving in 2025, having mastered the habits and strategies discussed this book.

Redefining Success: The Freedom to Live Life on Your Terms

Success means different things to different people, but true success is about freedom. I about having the financial resources, time, and mental clarity to live a life aligned with yo deepest values. In 2025, the path to this freedom lies in redefining wealth not as a numb in your bank account but as a holistic concept encompassing health, relationships, tim and financial security.

To redefine success, begin by reflecting on what truly matters to you. Are you chasing lifestyle dictated by societal expectations, or are you pursuing goals that genuinely ful you? For some, success might mean building a multimillion-dollar empire, while for othe could mean achieving financial independence to travel the world or spend quality time with loved ones.

Clarity is key. Write down your definition of success and break it into actionable steps. For example, if financial freedom is your goal, determine the amount of passive income needed to cover your expenses and identify strategies to achieve it, such as investments or building scalable income streams. If personal growth is part of your vision, commit to continuous learning through books, courses, and mentorships.

Embracing a Wealth-Conscious Mindset

A wealth-conscious mindset is not about greed; it's about abundance. It recognizes that the world is filled with opportunities to create value, and that wealth is a byproduct of solving problems for others. Shifting your perspective from scarcity to abundance unlocks a world of possibilities.

Many people unknowingly operate from a scarcity mindset. They see money as a finite resource, leading to fear-based decisions such as hoarding cash or avoiding investments. This mindset creates a cycle of stagnation. Conversely, an abundance mindset focuses on growth and expansion. It understands that money flows where value is created and that wealth multiplies when managed wisely.

To cultivate this mindset, start by reframing your relationship with money. Instead of viewing it as something to be feared or avoided, see it as a tool for empowerment. Develop habits like budgeting, saving, and investing, not out of fear but as acts of self-care and future-building.

Equally important is gratitude. Acknowledge and appreciate the resources you already have. Gratitude shifts your focus from lack to abundance, opening your mind to new opportunities. Practice daily gratitude journaling by listing three things you're thankful for, and watch how this simple habit transforms your perspective.

Overcoming Fear and Embracing Risk

Fear is the greatest enemy of success. Whether it's fear of failure, fear of rejection, or fear of the unknown, it keeps countless individuals stuck in their comfort zones, far from the life they desire. The truth is, growth and wealth-building require taking calculated risks. To succeed in 2025, you must learn to embrace uncertainty and see risk as a necessary ingredient for progress.

The first step in overcoming fear is understanding it. Fear is a natural response to perceived danger, but in modern life, it often arises from imagined scenarios rather than real threats. Recognize when fear is holding you back and challenge its validity. Ask yourself, "What's the worst that can happen?" Often, the worst-case scenario is far less catastrophic than your mind suggests.

Next, build a tolerance for discomfort. Success requires stepping into unfamiliar territory, whether it's launching a new business, investing in a volatile market, or learning a challenging skill. Start small by taking manageable risks and gradually increase your comfort zone. Celebrate your courage, even if the outcome isn't perfect.

Finally, reframe failure as feedback. Every successful individual has faced setbacks, b[ut] they view these as learning experiences rather than endpoints. Adopt the mantra, "I eith[er] win or learn," and let this perspective guide your journey.

The Importance of Habits and Consistency

Success is not built on grand gestures but on small, consistent actions. Your habits are t[he] foundation of your mindset, and cultivating the right ones can transform your life. F[or] instance, daily reading, regular exercise, and disciplined financial management are hab[its] that compound over time, leading to extraordinary results.

James Clear, in *Atomic Habits*, emphasizes the power of incremental improvements. If y[ou] improve by just 1% every day, these small gains add up to remarkable progress over a ye[ar]. Apply this principle to every area of your life. If you want to build wealth, commit to savi[ng] and investing a portion of your income consistently, even if the amounts seem small at fir[st]. If you want to enhance your mindset, dedicate time to personal development each da[y], whether through reading, meditation, or networking with like-minded individuals.

Accountability is crucial. Share your goals with a trusted friend, mentor, or community, a[nd] track your progress. Celebrate milestones along the way, no matter how minor they see[m]. Success is a journey, and every step forward is worth acknowledging.

Visualizing the Future: Thriving in 2025

Imagine yourself thriving in 2025. Picture a life where you wake up excited about the d[ay] ahead, free from financial worries and filled with purpose. This vision can become yo[ur] reality if you commit to shifting your mindset today.

Start by creating a vision board or a written manifesto outlining your goals for 202[5]. Include specific details about your ideal financial situation, lifestyle, and perso[nal] achievements. Revisit this vision regularly and let it inspire your daily actions.

Equally important is flexibility. While it's crucial to have a vision, life is unpredictable, a[nd] success often involves adapting to unforeseen circumstances. Stay open to n[ew] opportunities and be willing to pivot when necessary. Remember, resilience a[nd] adaptability are hallmarks of a successful mindset.

The journey to success, wealth, and freedom begins with your mindset. By shifting yo[ur] perspectives, embracing growth, and cultivating habits that support your goals, you c[an] achieve extraordinary results. The strategies outlined in this chapter are not theoretical[;] they are proven principles practiced by some of the most successful individuals in history[.]

As you move forward, remember that the power to change your life lies within you. In t[he] chapters ahead, we'll explore actionable strategies to build wealth, achieve freedom, a[nd] thrive in 2025. But the foundation is already laid. By mastering the mindset of succe[ss], you've taken the first and most critical step toward unlocking your potential.

Developing a Positive and Abundance Mindset to Achieve Success

Success is often thought of as the result of hard work, strategy, and opportunity. Wh[ile] these factors play a significant role, the foundation of lasting success lies in your mindset[. A] positive and abundance-oriented mindset can transform how you view challeng[es,] opportunities, and your potential, acting as a catalyst for growth and fulfillment. T[his] chapter delves into how you can cultivate such a mindset and provides actionable strategies supported by examples and data to help you unlock your full potential.

The Science of Positivity: Why Your Mindset Matters

Studies have shown that individuals with a positive mindset are more likely to achieve success. A groundbreaking study by Barbara Fredrickson at the University of North Carolina demonstrated that positivity broadens your sense of possibilities and enhances your ability to build new skills. This phenomenon, known as the *broaden-and-build theory*, underscores how positivity is not just a fleeting emotion but a powerful tool for personal and professional growth.

For example, entrepreneurs who maintain an optimistic outlook are better equipped to weather setbacks and find creative solutions. Consider Sara Blakely, the founder of Spanx. Before becoming a billionaire, she faced numerous rejections while pitching her product idea. Instead of dwelling on negativity, she reframed each "no" as a step closer to finding the right opportunity. Her positive mindset not only kept her motivated but also allowed her to remain open to innovative ideas.

Shifting from Scarcity to Abundance

One of the most profound shifts you can make is transitioning from a scarcity mindset to an abundance mindset. A scarcity mindset sees resources, opportunities, and success as finite, leading to fear-based decisions. Conversely, an abundance mindset recognizes that there is enough for everyone and focuses on growth, collaboration, and long-term thinking.

Take the example of businesses during economic downturns. Companies with a scarcity mindset might cut costs aggressively and avoid risks, often leading to stagnation. On the other hand, those with an abundance mindset invest in innovation and talent, positioning themselves for future growth. Apple, for instance, launched the iPod during a recession, which became a cornerstone of its resurgence. This bold move exemplified a belief in opportunities even during challenging times.

Developing an abundance mindset requires conscious effort. Start by reframing how you view competition. Instead of seeing competitors as threats, consider them as collaborators who can help expand the market. Networking events and industry conferences provide excellent opportunities to practice this mindset. For example, rather than guarding your ideas, share them openly and seek feedback. You may find that collaboration leads to unexpected partnerships and opportunities.

The Role of Gratitude in Cultivating Positivity

Gratitude is a cornerstone of a positive and abundance-oriented mindset. Research from the Greater Good Science Center at UC Berkeley reveals that individuals who practice gratitude consistently experience higher levels of happiness and reduced stress. Gratitude shifts your focus from what you lack to what you already have, fostering a sense of abundance.

For instance, billionaire investor Warren Buffett is known for his deep sense of gratitude. Despite his immense wealth, Buffett often emphasizes his appreciation for simple pleasures, such as spending time with family or enjoying a good book. This mindset not only keeps him grounded but also reinforces his long-term investment strategies, which rely on patience and trust.

To cultivate gratitude, consider starting a daily gratitude journal. Each morning or evening, write down three things you're thankful for. These could range from major achievements to small moments of joy. Over time, this practice trains your brain to focus on the positive, creating a ripple effect in your personal and professional life.

Visualization and the Power of Belief

Visualization is a powerful tool for developing an abundance mindset. When you vividly imagine your desired outcomes, you activate the same neural pathways as when you're physically working toward those goals. This process reinforces belief in your ability to succeed and primes your brain for action.

A compelling example comes from Olympic athletes who use visualization to enhance performance. Studies show that mentally rehearsing a routine can improve actual performance almost as much as physical practice. Similarly, visualizing your success—whether it's acing a presentation, achieving a financial milestone, or launching a new venture—can significantly boost your confidence and motivation.

Create a vision board that represents your goals. Include images, words, and symbols that resonate with your aspirations. Place it somewhere you'll see daily, serving as a constant reminder of your objectives. Additionally, practice guided visualization exercises. Spend a few minutes each day imagining yourself achieving your goals in vivid detail, focusing on the emotions, actions, and outcomes involved.

Overcoming Negativity Bias

The human brain is wired to focus on negativity as a survival mechanism. This negativity bias can make it challenging to maintain a positive mindset, especially in the face of setbacks. However, by consciously countering this bias, you can train your mind to focus on opportunities and solutions rather than problems.

A practical strategy is the *three-to-one ratio*, suggested by positive psychology researchers. For every negative thought or experience, counterbalance it with three positive ones. For instance, if you're frustrated by a project delay, remind yourself of three things that are progressing well. Over time, this practice rewires your brain to focus on the positive.

Consider the story of Thomas Edison, who famously conducted over 1,000 unsuccessful experiments before inventing the lightbulb. When asked about his "failures," Edison reframed them as learning experiences, saying, "I have not failed. I've just found 10,000 ways that won't work." His ability to focus on progress rather than setbacks exemplifies the power of overcoming negativity bias.

Building Positive Habits for Success

Habits play a critical role in shaping your mindset. By embedding positive practices into your daily routine, you create a supportive environment for growth and success. One highly effective habit is mindfulness, which involves staying present and fully engaged in the moment.

Research from Harvard University indicates that mindfulness improves focus, reduces stress, and enhances decision-making—key traits for success. Tech leaders like Satya Nadella, CEO of Microsoft, attribute part of their success to mindfulness practices, which help them navigate complex challenges with clarity and composure.

incorporate mindfulness into your routine through meditation, deep breathing exercises, or simply pausing to observe your surroundings. Start small, dedicating just five minutes a day to this practice, and gradually increase as it becomes part of your lifestyle.

Another transformative habit is goal-setting. Write down your short-term and long-term goals and break them into actionable steps. Studies show that people who write down their goals are 42% more likely to achieve them. For example, if your goal is to increase your income, outline specific actions such as acquiring new skills, networking, or pursuing additional revenue streams.

Data-Driven Benefits of a Positive and Abundance Mindset

The impact of a positive mindset isn't just anecdotal—it's supported by data. A 2019 study published in the *Journal of Personality and Social Psychology* found that optimistic individuals were 40% more likely to experience financial success and 30% less likely to encounter health-related setbacks. Furthermore, businesses led by optimistic leaders outperform their peers, as positivity fosters resilience, creativity, and effective teamwork.

Another compelling statistic comes from Gallup's *State of the Global Workplace* report, which highlights that employees who feel valued and optimistic are 17% more productive and have 41% lower absenteeism rates. These findings emphasize that positivity is not just a "nice-to-have" trait but a critical driver of performance and success.

Real-Life Examples of Abundance in Action

The story of Oprah Winfrey serves as an inspiring example of an abundance mindset. Born into poverty, Oprah faced numerous obstacles, including abuse and discrimination. Despite these challenges, she cultivated a belief in her potential and focused on creating value. Her mindset allowed her to seize opportunities, build meaningful connections, and ultimately become one of the most influential figures in the world.

Similarly, Elon Musk's success stems from his ability to think abundantly. Rather than viewing space exploration or renewable energy as insurmountable challenges, Musk sees them as opportunities to push humanity forward. His companies, Tesla and SpaceX, exemplify how an abundance mindset drives innovation and global impact.

Developing a positive and abundance-oriented mindset is a transformative journey. By shifting from scarcity to abundance, practicing gratitude, visualizing success, and building supportive habits, you can unlock new levels of achievement and fulfillment. The examples and data presented here highlight that positivity is not just a personal choice but a proven pathway to success.

As you apply these principles, remember that change takes time and consistency. Each step, no matter how small, brings you closer to a life of abundance. By committing to this mindset, you'll not only achieve your goals but also inspire others to do the same, creating a ripple effect of positivity and growth.

Summary Table: Developing a Positive and Abundance Mindset

Key Principle	Description	Example	Supporting Data
The Science of Positivity	Positivity broadens perspectives and enhances skill-building.	Sara Blakely reframed rejections as learning opportunities, leading to Spanx's success.	Positive individuals are 40% more likely to achieve financial success (*Journal of Personality and Social Psychology*, 2019).
Shifting from Scarcity to Abundance	Recognizing opportunities as limitless fosters growth and innovation.	Apple launched the iPod during a recession, demonstrating long-term vision.	Companies with abundant mindsets outperform competitors during economic downturns.
Gratitude as a Foundation	Focusing on what you have increases happiness and reduces stress.	Warren Buffett practices gratitude for simple joys, reinforcing long-term investment strategies.	Gratitude boosts happiness and reduces stress (*Greater Good Science Center*).
Visualization and Belief	Mentally rehearsing success activates neural pathways, boosting confidence and performance.	Olympic athletes use visualization to enhance physical performance.	Visualization improves performance almost as much as physical practice (sports psychology studies).
Overcoming Negativity Bias	Counter negative thoughts with positive reinforcement to rewire your brain.	Thomas Edison reframed 1,000 "failures" as steps toward the lightbulb invention.	The *three-to-one ratio* helps balance negative thoughts with positivity (positive psychology research).
Building Positive Habits	Embedding mindfulness and goal-setting into daily routines fosters clarity and focus.	Satya Nadella uses mindfulness to navigate challenges effectively at Microsoft.	Mindfulness improves focus and reduces stress (*Harvard University* research).
The Data-Driven Impact of Positivity	Optimism enhances financial success, health, and productivity.	Businesses led by optimistic leaders show higher innovation and teamwork.	Optimistic people are 30% less likely to face health setbacks (*Journal of Personality and Social Psychology*, 2019).
Real-Life Abundance Examples	Leaders leverage abundance thinking to overcome obstacles and innovate.	Oprah Winfrey and Elon Musk pursued opportunities with an abundant mindset.	Employees with optimism are 17% more productive (*Gallup's State of the Global Workplace* report).

CHAPTER 2: BUILDING WEALTH: STRATEGIES TO MULTIPLY YOUR INCOME STREAMS

Building wealth isn't just about working harder; it's about working smarter. In today's fast-paced, hyper-connected world, the key to financial success lies in diversification and adopting strategies that align with the ever-evolving economic landscape. Wealth-building is no longer restricted to traditional savings accounts or long-term investments; it requires a mindset shift toward actively creating multiple income streams. This chapter dives into proven strategies to multiply your income, build financial security, and lay the foundation for long-term success.

Understanding the Power of Diversified Income Streams

The days of relying on a single income source are long gone. Whether you're an employee, entrepreneur, or freelancer, depending solely on one paycheck is a risky proposition in an unpredictable economy. Diversification is the cornerstone of wealth-building. By creating multiple income streams, you protect yourself from market fluctuations, industry downturns, or unexpected job loss. More importantly, diversification accelerates your financial growth, enabling you to achieve goals like early retirement, debt elimination, or funding big dreams.

A diversified income portfolio can include a mix of active income, where you exchange time for money, and passive income, which requires upfront effort but eventually generates revenue with minimal ongoing involvement. The ideal strategy balances these two to create both stability and scalability.

Step 1: Identify Your Financial Goals and Prioritize Action

Before diving into income diversification, it's crucial to outline your financial objectives. Are you looking to save for a major life event, invest in real estate, or build a retirement fund? Clear goals act as your North Star, helping you allocate resources wisely and maintain focus on what matters most.

Begin by assessing your current income and expenses. Understand where your money is going and identify areas where you can cut back to free up resources for investment. Start small—set achievable milestones to build momentum. For example, saving $500 a month could eventually fund a real estate venture or a side hustle. With clear goals, even modest beginnings can snowball into significant financial gains.

Step 2: Leverage Your Expertise to Create Active Income

Many people underestimate the value of their skills. Your expertise, whether in graphic design, writing, coding, or consulting, can be a lucrative avenue for creating additional active income streams. Freelancing platforms like Upwork, Fiverr, or LinkedIn are goldmines for monetizing your talents. By dedicating even a few hours a week, you can establish a steady side income that complements your primary job.

Another way to leverage expertise is through online courses and digital products. Platforms like Teachable and Gumroad allow you to package your knowledge into downloadable resources or video lessons. For instance, a graphic designer can create tutorials on mastering Adobe Photoshop, while a fitness coach might sell personalized workout plans. Digital products are scalable, offering significant earning potential with minimal ongoing effort once established.

Step 3: Explore Passive Income Opportunities

Passive income is often heralded as the holy grail of wealth-building. While it requires upfront work, it's an indispensable part of any wealth strategy. Real estate investments are among the most popular avenues for passive income. Rental properties, REITs (Real Estate Investment Trusts), or even short-term rentals on platforms like Airbnb provide consistent returns with relatively low involvement once operational.

Dividend-paying stocks are another effective tool for passive income. Companies that distribute regular dividends offer a reliable stream of income while growing your wealth over time. Similarly, investing in index funds or ETFs (Exchange-Traded Funds) ensures diversification, reducing risk while steadily building wealth.

If investing isn't your immediate focus, consider licensing your intellectual property, such as photographs, music, or writing. Websites like Shutterstock and Kindle Direct Publishing allow creators to earn royalties indefinitely, making your creative efforts pay off long after the initial work is complete.

Step 4: Harness the Gig Economy

The gig economy is thriving, presenting countless opportunities for side hustles. Platforms like Uber, DoorDash, and TaskRabbit let you turn underutilized resources—like your car or spare time—into income. While these gigs may not lead to long-term wealth, they can provide immediate cash flow to fund other ventures.

Gig economy platforms are also an excellent way to test entrepreneurial ideas. For instance, starting as a freelance consultant on a platform like Upwork can help you refine your services before launching a full-fledged business. The low entry barriers make the gig economy a risk-free testing ground for bigger financial plans.

Step 5: Invest in Real Estate for Stability and Growth

Real estate remains one of the most reliable wealth-building strategies. From purchasing rental properties to flipping homes, real estate offers a range of income-generating opportunities. Start small with residential properties in emerging neighborhoods where the cost of entry is lower but the growth potential is high. Over time, you can scale up to commercial properties or diversify into real estate crowdfunding platforms like Fundrise or RealtyMogul.

For those without the capital to buy property outright, house hacking is a popular alternative. By renting out a portion of your home or investing in multi-unit properties, you can offset mortgage costs while building equity.

Step 6: Build a Digital Presence to Scale Income Streams

In today's digital-first world, an online presence is essential for scaling income streams. Whether you're selling products, offering services, or promoting content, platforms like Instagram, YouTube, and TikTok enable you to reach a global audience. Social media is more than a marketing tool—it's an income generator. From sponsorships to ad revenue, a robust digital presence opens doors to countless monetization opportunities.

Blogging is another effective way to earn passive income. By creating valuable, niche-specific content, you can attract an audience and monetize through affiliate marketing, sponsored posts, or ad placements. Tools like Google AdSense and Amazon Associates make it simple to start earning through your website.

Step 7: Start a Business or Scale an Existing One

Entrepreneurship is one of the most rewarding ways to build wealth. Whether you're launching a side hustle or scaling an existing business, the opportunities are endless. E-commerce, for example, continues to grow exponentially. Platforms like Shopify or Etsy make it easy to set up a store and reach customers worldwide. The key to success is identifying a niche, providing value, and delivering exceptional customer experiences.

For established business owners, scaling operations through automation, outsourcing, or franchising can significantly increase income potential. Consider reinvesting profits into expanding your product line, enhancing marketing efforts, or optimizing processes to achieve exponential growth.

Step 8: Prioritize Networking and Collaboration

Wealth-building isn't a solo journey. Surrounding yourself with the right people—mentors, peers, and collaborators—can accelerate your success. Attend industry events, join online forums, or participate in local meetups to expand your network. Building relationships with like-minded individuals not only provides support but also opens doors to joint ventures, partnerships, and investment opportunities.

Collaboration is particularly effective for scaling income streams. For instance, teaming up with an influencer to promote your product or co-authoring an online course can double your audience and revenue. Partnerships reduce risk while amplifying returns, making them a powerful tool for wealth creation.

Step 9: Automate and Optimize Financial Systems

Finally, automation is the secret weapon for managing and multiplying income streams efficiently. Use technology to your advantage by setting up systems that handle recurring tasks like budgeting, invoicing, and investing. Apps like Mint, YNAB (You Need a Budget), o Robo-advisors like Betterment simplify financial management, ensuring you stay on track with minimal effort.

Optimization is equally important. Regularly review your income streams to identify underperforming assets or ventures. Reallocate resources to high-performing areas, streamline operations, and eliminate inefficiencies. A well-optimized system not only saves time but also maximizes profitability.

The Mindset of Wealth-Builders

At the heart of wealth-building lies a mindset of growth, resilience, and adaptability. Challenges and failures are inevitable, but those who persevere and continuously seek opportunities ultimately succeed. Cultivate habits like lifelong learning, disciplined saving, and strategic risk-taking. Stay informed about market trends, technological advancements, and emerging industries to stay ahead of the curve.

Wealth-building is not a one-time effort; it's a dynamic, ongoing process. By diversifying income streams, leveraging technology, and maintaining a proactive mindset, you can achieve financial freedom, security, and a lifestyle that thrives in 2025 and beyond. The strategies outlined in this chapter are not just about accumulating wealth but about creating a sustainable and fulfilling financial future.

Proven Methods for Generating Passive Income, Smart Investments, and Entrepreneurship

Building wealth is a combination of strategic planning, leveraging opportunities, and consistent execution. While active income provides the foundation for financial security, true financial freedom often comes from diversifying into passive income, making intelligent investments, and exploring entrepreneurial ventures. Let's explore proven methods to achieve these goals, supported by real-world examples and actionable insights

Understanding Passive Income: The Gateway to Financial Freedom

Passive income refers to money earned with minimal effort after an initial setup. The allure lies in its ability to generate ongoing revenue, freeing you to focus on other ventures or enjoy life. Passive income isn't "easy money"—it requires planning, effort, and in some cases, investment—but it's a powerful tool for financial growth.

Real Estate Investments

Real estate remains one of the most reliable methods for passive income. A standout example is Grant Cardone, a renowned real estate mogul. Through Cardone Capital, he has acquired multi-family apartment complexes, generating millions in annual rental income while allowing others to invest passively.

For individuals starting out, house hacking is an accessible entry point. Purchase a multi-unit property, live in one unit, and rent out the others. This strategy often offsets mortgage costs and builds equity. Platforms like **Fundrise** and **Roofstock** make real estate investments accessible to those without substantial capital, offering options like REITs (Real Estate Investment Trusts) with returns averaging **6-10% annually**.

Dividend-Paying Stocks

Investing in dividend-paying stocks is another proven method. Companies like **Coca-Cola**, **Procter & Gamble**, and **Johnson & Johnson** have a track record of consistently paying dividends. For instance, someone holding $100,000 worth of Coca-Cola shares with a **3% annual dividend yield** would earn $3,000 annually without selling the stock.

To enhance returns, reinvest dividends using a Dividend Reinvestment Plan (DRIP), which compounds growth over time. Tools like **Robinhood** or **Charles Schwab** simplify the process, making it accessible even for beginners.

Digital Products and Online Courses

Digital products are highly scalable. Think about Pat Flynn, who built a passive income empire by creating online courses and eBooks. His course **"Smart Podcast Player"** earns over **$200,000 annually**, proving that expertise can translate into significant revenue.

Platforms like **Teachable**, **Udemy**, or **Kajabi** enable creators to monetize their skills. A graphic designer might sell Adobe Photoshop tutorials, while a marketer could offer courses on Facebook advertising. Once uploaded, these courses generate revenue indefinitely, requiring little ongoing effort.

Smart Investments: Making Your Money Work for You

Investing intelligently is the backbone of wealth-building. By aligning your investments with your risk tolerance and financial goals, you can grow your portfolio significantly over time.

Stock Market Investing

The stock market is one of the most accessible ways to build wealth. Warren Buffett, one of the most successful investors, advocates investing in index funds like the **S&P 500**, which has delivered an average annual return of **10% over the past century**.

For beginners, dollar-cost averaging (DCA) is a low-risk strategy. Instead of investing a lump sum, allocate a fixed amount regularly to buy stocks or ETFs, smoothing out market volatility.

Cryptocurrency and Blockchain

Cryptocurrency is a high-risk, high-reward investment. Bitcoin, for example, saw a meteoric rise from **$1,000 in 2017 to over $60,000 in 2021**. While the market is volatile, long-term strategies like staking—where you earn rewards for holding crypto in a wallet—can provide steady income.

Platforms like **Coinbase** or **Binance** make staking accessible. For instance, staking **Ethereum** can yield returns of **4-8% annually**, making it an attractive option for tech-savvy investors.

6. Peer-to-Peer Lending

Peer-to-peer (P2P) lending platforms like **LendingClub** and **Prosper** allow you to lend money to individuals or small businesses in exchange for interest payments. With average returns ranging from **4-7%**, P2P lending diversifies your income sources while contributing to economic growth.

Entrepreneurship: Building Scalable Income Streams

Entrepreneurship offers limitless earning potential and the opportunity to make a significant impact. Successful businesses often start with identifying a niche and solving problems for a specific audience.

7. E-commerce and Dropshipping

E-commerce continues to boom, with global online sales reaching **$5.7 trillion in 2022**. Shopify, Amazon, and Etsy provide platforms to sell products with minimal upfront investment. Dropshipping, in particular, eliminates inventory costs by allowing sellers to ship products directly from suppliers to customers.

Consider Sarah Chrisp, who built a six-figure dropshipping business with products source from AliExpress. Her store specializes in niche products, demonstrating how targeted marketing and quality service can yield massive returns.

8. Subscription-Based Models

Subscription businesses thrive on recurring revenue. Netflix revolutionized this model in entertainment, and smaller-scale entrepreneurs have followed suit in various industries. For example, meal kit companies like **Blue Apron** or curated boxes like **Birchbox** offer convenience while ensuring consistent income.

Launching a subscription service in your area of expertise—whether fitness plans, exclusive content, or software tools—can create predictable revenue streams. Platforms like **Patreon** help creators monetize content through monthly memberships, making it easy to start small and scale gradually.

9. Franchising

Buying a franchise allows you to leverage a proven business model while minimizing startup risks. Brands like **McDonald's**, **Subway**, and **Chick-fil-A** are known for their consistent profitability. For instance, a Chick-fil-A franchise typically generates **$4.5 million annually** per store, far exceeding industry averages.

While initial costs can be steep, financing options and partnerships often make franchising an attainable venture. Aspiring entrepreneurs should research franchise opportunities in growing sectors like health, tech, or eco-friendly products.

Case Study: Elon Musk and the Power of Diversification

Elon Musk exemplifies the power of diversification. From PayPal to Tesla, SpaceX, and SolarCity, Musk has leveraged entrepreneurial ventures to amass a fortune of over **$300 billion**. Each business focuses on different industries—finance, automotive, aerospace, and renewable energy—reducing dependency on any single income source.

His journey highlights the importance of reinvesting profits into innovative projects, embracing calculated risks, and continuously exploring new opportunities. Entrepreneurs and investors can draw inspiration from Musk's ability to think big while executing with precision.

Scaling Your Efforts: Automation and Optimization

As you diversify income streams, automation becomes crucial for managing growth effectively. Tools like **Zapier**, **QuickBooks**, and **HubSpot** automate tasks like accounting, customer follow-ups, and marketing campaigns, freeing time to focus on strategic expansion.

Outsourcing

Outsourcing tasks allows you to scale operations without overextending yourself. Tim Ferriss, author of *The 4-Hour Workweek*, advocates delegating non-core tasks to virtual assistants or freelancers, enabling entrepreneurs to focus on high-impact activities. Websites like **Upwork** and **Fiverr** make finding skilled professionals simple and cost-effective.

Licensing Intellectual Property

Licensing your creations, whether music, books, or patents, generates royalties over time. For instance, J.K. Rowling earns millions annually through *Harry Potter* licensing agreements, proving the immense potential of intellectual property. Even small-scale creators can benefit by licensing designs to platforms like **Redbubble** or **Zazzle**.

Leveraging Technology for Exponential Growth

Building Apps or SaaS Products

The software-as-a-service (SaaS) market is booming, expected to reach **$307 billion by 2026**. Entrepreneurs like Tobias Lütke, founder of Shopify, have capitalized on this trend, creating scalable platforms that empower others while generating significant revenue. If you lack technical skills, consider outsourcing development or collaborating with a developer to bring your idea to life. Subscription-based apps or tools addressing specific pain points—like productivity trackers or financial planners—can provide consistent income.

Key Metrics to Track for Wealth Growth

1. **Cash Flow**: Monitor monthly income and expenses to ensure a positive cash flow.
2. **ROI (Return on Investment)**: Evaluate the profitability of your investments or ventures.
3. **Diversification Ratio**: Aim for a balanced portfolio to mitigate risks.

By tracking these metrics, you can make informed decisions, optimize performance, and maximize returns.

Creating wealth isn't about luck—it's about leveraging proven methods, staying adaptable and maintaining discipline. By embracing passive income opportunities, making smart investments, and pursuing entrepreneurial ventures, you set the stage for financial freedom and long-term prosperity.

These strategies, coupled with consistent learning and execution, ensure you're not just building wealth for yourself but creating a legacy that impacts future generations. Now is the time to take action—success starts with the first step.

CHAPTER 3: FREEDOM THROUGH FINANCIAL INDEPENDENCE: MASTERING YOUR MONEY

Are you living to work, or working to live? Have you ever wondered what it truly means to be financially independent? And most importantly, are you ready to take control of your money and create a life of freedom and abundance?

These three questions cut to the heart of what financial independence represents. It's not just about money; it's about creating choices, living on your terms, and achieving the freedom to pursue the life you've always envisioned. In this chapter, we will uncover the secrets of mastering your money, demystify the principles of financial independence, and equip you with practical strategies to turn your dreams into reality.

The Meaning of Financial Independence

Financial independence is often misunderstood as being "rich," but it is so much more than that. True financial independence is about **having enough wealth to cover your living expenses without relying on active work**. Imagine waking up every day with the ability to choose how to spend your time—not dictated by the need to earn a paycheck but driven by your passions, relationships, and goals.

This shift is not just about dollars and cents; it's a mindset transformation. To begin this journey, you must first examine your relationship with money. Are you controlling it, or is it controlling you? Financial independence starts with this foundational self-awareness.

Step 1: Define Your "Why"

Before diving into strategies, ask yourself: **Why do you want to achieve financial independence?** For some, it's the desire to spend more time with family. For others, it's the dream of traveling the world or starting a passion project. Clarity in your "why" serves as a guiding star, keeping you focused and motivated through the ups and downs of your financial journey.

Your "why" will also dictate your timeline and approach. A young professional aiming for early retirement might prioritize aggressive saving and investment strategies, while someone later in life may focus on debt elimination and income optimization.

Step 2: Assess Your Current Financial Health

Financial independence starts with a clear picture of where you stand today. Begin by calculating your **net worth**—the total of your assets (savings, investments, property) minus your liabilities (debt). This number represents your financial baseline.

Next, analyze your spending habits. Most people underestimate how much they spend on non-essential items like dining out, subscriptions, or impulse purchases. Use budgeting tools or apps to track every dollar for a month. This process may surprise you, but it's crucial to understand where your money goes.

Step 3: Master the Art of Budgeting

Budgeting isn't about restrictions; it's about empowerment. A solid budget is a tool that allows you to allocate your resources intentionally toward what matters most. Follow the **50/30/20 rule** as a starting point:

- **50% for needs** (housing, food, utilities).
- **30% for wants** (entertainment, hobbies).
- **20% for savings and debt repayment.**

If financial independence is your goal, consider flipping this rule to prioritize savings and investments. Every dollar you save today is a step closer to a future where you control your time.

Step 4: Break Free from Debt

Debt is one of the most significant barriers to financial independence. High-interest debt, like credit cards, can keep you trapped in a cycle of payments. The first step to freedom is to attack debt with a plan. Two popular methods are:

1. **The Snowball Method:** Pay off the smallest debt first to build momentum and motivation.
2. **The Avalanche Method:** Focus on debts with the highest interest rate to minimize costs.

Whichever method you choose, consistency is key. Every debt paid off brings you closer to financial freedom.

Step 5: Build an Emergency Fund

Life is unpredictable. An emergency fund acts as a financial safety net, preventing you from falling into debt when unexpected expenses arise. Aim to save **three to six months' worth of living expenses**. Start small, and automate your savings to make it a habit.

Step 6: Invest in Your Future

Saving money is essential, but saving alone won't lead to financial independence. To build lasting wealth, you must **invest**. The power of compound interest allows your money to grow exponentially over time. Start by understanding the basic investment vehicles:

- **Stock Market:** Offers high potential returns over the long term. Invest in diversified index funds to minimize risk.
- **Real Estate:** Provides both passive income and asset appreciation.
- **Retirement Accounts:** Maximize contributions to tax-advantaged accounts like 401(k)s or IRAs.

The earlier you start, the more time your money has to grow. Even small amounts invested consistently can yield significant results over decades.

Step 7: Cultivate Multiple Income Streams

Relying on a single income source is risky in today's volatile economy. Financially independent individuals often have **multiple streams of income**, such as:

- **Side hustles** or freelance work.
- **Passive income** from investments, rental properties, or royalties.
- **Entrepreneurship**, building businesses that generate revenue even when you're not actively involved.

Diversifying your income reduces financial vulnerability and accelerates your journey to independence.

Step 8: Adopt a Long-Term Perspective

Financial independence isn't achieved overnight. It requires patience, discipline, and a long-term perspective. Avoid the temptation of get-rich-quick schemes or risky investments. Focus on sustainable growth and make decisions that align with your goals.

The Power of Financial Freedom

Imagine the possibilities when financial independence becomes your reality. You could:

- Pursue a career or business driven by passion, not necessity.
- Spend more quality time with loved ones.
- Explore the world, immerse yourself in new cultures, or even move abroad.
- Give back to your community or support causes you care about.

The true power of financial independence lies in the freedom it provides—the freedom to live intentionally and without fear.

Overcoming Common Barriers

It's natural to feel overwhelmed or doubt your ability to achieve financial independence. Here are common obstacles and strategies to overcome them:

- **Low Income:** Focus on increasing your earning potential through skills development, networking, or career advancement.
- **High Expenses:** Identify areas where you can cut costs without sacrificing quality of life.
- **Lack of Knowledge:** Educate yourself on personal finance through books, podcasts, or courses.

Remember, every small step forward matters. Consistency and persistence will carry you through challenges.

Taking Action Today

Don't wait for the "perfect moment" to start your financial independence journey. Begin today, no matter where you are financially. Start by implementing one strategy from this chapter—whether it's creating a budget, setting up an investment account, or tackling a small debt.

Each step you take builds momentum, bringing you closer to a life of freedom and abundance. As you progress, you'll discover that mastering your money is not just about numbers; it's about empowering yourself to create the life you deserve.

Financial independence is a journey, not a destination. Along the way, you'll face challenges, celebrate milestones, and gain invaluable wisdom. Remember that this path is not just about achieving wealth but about reclaiming your time, pursuing your passions, and living with purpose.

As you reflect on the questions posed at the beginning of this chapter, ask yourself: **What steps will you take today to master your money and build a life of freedom?**

Master Your Personal Finances, Eliminate Debt, and Achieve Financial Independence

Have you ever felt like your money controls you, rather than the other way around? Do you wonder why some people thrive financially while others barely scrape by, despite similar incomes? And finally, what would your life look like if you were financially free—free from debt, stress, and limitations?

In this chapter, we'll uncover practical strategies to master personal finances, eliminate debt, and build the foundation for financial independence. Along the way, we'll explore a case study of a success story and cautionary lessons from a high-profile failure to highlight the real-world application of these principles.

The Foundation of Financial Mastery

At the core of financial success lies one fundamental truth: **it's not how much you earn but how you manage what you have.** Wealthy individuals and financially independent people often excel at one key skill—**discipline.** They live intentionally, track their finances, and prioritize long-term stability over short-term gratification.

Step 1: Know Your Numbers

The first step in taking control of your finances is understanding where you stand. This means:

- **Assessing your net worth**: Total assets (savings, investments, property) minus liabilities (debts).
- **Tracking your cash flow**: How much money comes in and goes out monthly.

By understanding your financial position, you can pinpoint areas to improve and start building a roadmap toward independence.

Step 2: Create a Budget

A budget is more than just a list of numbers; it's a blueprint for your financial life. Consider the **zero-based budgeting method**, where every dollar has a purpose—whether for essentials, investments, or fun. Allocate your income intentionally, ensuring a portion is always directed toward savings and debt repayment.

Step 3: Break Free from Debt

Debt is often the most significant barrier to financial independence. High-interest debts, like credit cards or payday loans, are particularly destructive, as they compound over time and can quickly spiral out of control.

To tackle debt, adopt one of two proven strategies:

1. **The Snowball Method**: Start by paying off the smallest debts first to build psychological momentum.
2. **The Avalanche Method**: Prioritize debts with the highest interest rates to minimize total costs.

Both methods work as long as you stay consistent. Combine these efforts with a commitment to avoid taking on new debt, and you'll eventually dig yourself out of the financial hole.

The Success Story: Elon Musk

Elon Musk, one of the wealthiest and most influential entrepreneurs of our time, wasn't always financially stable. In fact, Musk's journey toward financial success involved extraordinary risks, frugality, and a clear vision.

In 2008, Musk faced near-total financial ruin. His two ventures, Tesla and SpaceX, were on the brink of collapse, and he had burned through most of his personal fortune trying to keep them afloat. Instead of giving up or seeking bankruptcy protection, Musk doubled down. He sold his assets, moved into a modest rental, and used his last $20 million to keep both companies alive.

...st forward to today, Tesla and SpaceX are industry leaders, and Musk is one of the richest ...dividuals globally. His story exemplifies how careful financial discipline, combined with ...nwavering belief and strategic risk-taking, can lead to unparalleled success.

...y Lessons from Musk's Story:

- **Live Below Your Means**: Musk famously cut personal expenses to save his companies.
- **Prioritize Investments in Growth**: He focused on long-term vision rather than short-term luxuries.
- **Take Calculated Risks**: While risky, Musk's decisions were backed by meticulous planning and data.

...ne Failure: Bernie Madoff

... contrast to Musk's disciplined and visionary financial practices, Bernie Madoff's story is ... cautionary tale of greed and financial mismanagement.

...adoff was a former NASDAQ chairman and founder of a wealth management firm that ...romised extraordinary returns. However, it was later revealed to be the largest Ponzi ...heme in history, defrauding thousands of investors of nearly $65 billion.

...nlike Musk, who risked his own money to build a legitimate empire, Madoff relied on ...eceit, misused client funds, and perpetuated a financial illusion. When the 2008 financial ...isis hit, investors demanded their money back, but Madoff's scheme collapsed, leading to ...s arrest and a 150-year prison sentence.

...y Lessons from Madoff's Story:

- **Avoid Get-Rich-Quick Schemes**: If an investment seems too good to be true, it probably is.
- **Value Transparency**: Trustworthy financial practices are built on honesty and accountability.
- **Understand Where Your Money Goes**: Never invest in something you don't fully understand.

...ne Journey to Financial Independence

...chieving financial independence is a marathon, not a sprint. It requires a combination of ...bits, mindset shifts, and intentional decision-making. Here's how you can apply the ...ssons from both Musk and Madoff to your own financial journey:

...p 4: Build an Emergency Fund

...n emergency fund is your first line of defense against financial instability. Aim to save at ...ast three to six months' worth of living expenses in a liquid, easily accessible account. ...is fund prevents minor emergencies from derailing your progress and helps you avoid ...lling back into debt.

...p 5: Invest Wisely

...o achieve financial independence, you need to grow your money. Start by understanding ...sic investment vehicles:

- **Stocks**: High potential for growth over the long term.
- **Bonds**: Provide stability and predictable returns.
- **Real Estate**: Offers passive income and asset appreciation.
- **Index Funds and ETFs**: Diversified investments with lower risk.

...ollow Musk's example by focusing on long-term growth rather than chasing quick returns. ...emember to diversify your portfolio to spread risk.

Step 6: Create Multiple Income Streams

Relying on a single income source is risky in today's volatile economy. Explore ways to generate additional income, such as:
- Starting a side hustle or freelancing.
- Investing in dividend-paying stocks or real estate.
- Monetizing hobbies or skills, like writing, teaching, or consulting.

Diversifying your income streams ensures financial stability and accelerates your path to independence.

Mindset Shifts for Financial Freedom

Success with personal finances isn't just about numbers—it's about mindset. Consider these shifts to support your journey:

1. **Delay Gratification**: Financial independence requires sacrifices in the short term to achieve greater rewards later.
2. **Adopt an Abundance Mentality**: Believe that wealth is accessible and that you have the power to create it.
3. **Learn Continuously**: The more you understand about personal finance and investing, the better decisions you'll make.

The Ripple Effect of Financial Freedom

Financial independence isn't just about personal gain; it's about creating opportunities for others. When you're no longer burdened by financial stress, you can:
- Support your family and community.
- Invest in causes or businesses you care about.
- Pursue meaningful projects that inspire you.

Both Elon Musk and Bernie Madoff illustrate how financial decisions have far-reaching consequences—not just for individuals but for society as a whole. By managing your money with integrity and purpose, you can contribute to a legacy of positive impact.

Taking the First Step

No matter where you stand today—whether buried in debt or just starting to save—you have the power to transform your financial future. Start with small, consistent steps:
- Review your budget and cut unnecessary expenses.
- Set up an emergency fund and automate contributions.
- Begin investing, even if it's just a small amount each month.

Each step brings you closer to financial independence and the freedom to live life on your terms.

Mastering personal finances, eliminating debt, and achieving financial independence are within your reach. The stories of Elon Musk and Bernie Madoff reveal the stark contrasts between disciplined wealth-building and destructive financial behavior.

The path forward requires intentional action, a long-term mindset, and the courage to make difficult choices. But the rewards—freedom, stability, and the ability to live a life of purpose—are more than worth the effort.

Ask yourself again: **Are you ready to control your money and create a future of financial independence?** The answer lies in the steps you take starting today.

Question	Key Statistic	Insight for Readers
1. Do you know your current financial position, including your net worth and monthly cash flow?	78% of Americans live paycheck to paycheck, regardless of income level.	Understanding your financial position is the first step toward financial independence.
2. How much of your income are you allocating toward savings or debt repayment?	The average savings rate in the U.S. is only 5.1% of disposable income, far below the recommended 20%.	Prioritizing savings and debt repayment can significantly accelerate your path to financial stability.
3. Are you diversifying your income streams to protect against economic uncertainty?	65% of millionaires have at least three sources of income, compared to one for the average person.	Building multiple income streams provides financial resilience and creates opportunities for growth.

CHAPTER 4: THRIVING IN 2025: EMBRACING CHANGE AND CAPITALIZING ON TRENDS

The year 2025 is not merely a marker on a calendar; it represents a turning point in human history. As technological advancements accelerate, global dynamics shift, and the collective mindset evolves, individuals and businesses alike are presented with a choice: adapt and thrive or resist and falter. Thriving in 2025 requires more than passive observation—it demands proactive engagement with change, leveraging emerging trends, and adopting a forward-thinking mindset. This chapter delves into actionable strategies to embrace the inevitable shifts and capitalize on the trends shaping our world.

The Power of Adaptability in a Rapidly Changing World

Adaptability has always been a cornerstone of success, but in 2025, its importance has reached unprecedented levels. The pace of change, fueled by advancements in artificial intelligence (AI), automation, and quantum computing, has created an environment where yesterday's solutions are quickly becoming obsolete. This new era rewards those who can pivot effectively, learn continuously, and remain flexible in the face of uncertainty.

Adaptability begins with cultivating a mindset of openness. In 2025, lifelong learning is not just a buzzword—it is a survival strategy. Whether it's enrolling in micro-credential programs, attending virtual workshops, or participating in professional networks, individuals and businesses must prioritize education to stay ahead. The most successful individuals will not merely react to change; they will anticipate it, aligning their goals and strategies with the emerging realities of the future.

Consider the case of automation. While many industries have faced displacement due to robotic technologies, others have flourished by reimagining roles and responsibilities. For example, in healthcare, AI-driven diagnostics have augmented the capabilities of practitioners, allowing them to focus on patient care rather than administrative tasks. Similarly, in retail, companies leveraging predictive analytics and personalized marketing have outpaced competitors clinging to traditional models. The lesson is clear: those who adapt to change instead of resisting it position themselves for long-term success.

Emerging Trends That Will Define 2025

To thrive in 2025, it is essential to understand the key trends shaping the global landscape. These trends are not fleeting fads; they represent foundational shifts with long-term implications.

1. **Decentralization and Web3 Revolution**
   The transition to a decentralized internet, often referred to as Web3, is transforming the way we interact online. Blockchain technology has moved beyond cryptocurrencies to power decentralized finance (DeFi), smart contracts, and tokenized economies. Individuals who educate themselves on blockchain applications and explore opportunities in decentralized platforms will gain a competitive edge.
2. **Green Tech and Sustainable Solutions**
   As climate change concerns escalate, green technology has moved from a niche sector to the forefront of innovation. Companies embracing sustainability—whether through renewable energy, carbon offsetting, or eco-friendly manufacturing—are not only meeting regulatory requirements but also winning consumer loyalty. Entrepreneurs and investors should seek opportunities in sectors such as electric vehicles (EVs), clean energy, and circular economies to align with this global shift.
3. **The Metaverse and Virtual Reality (VR)**
   The metaverse is no longer a concept confined to science fiction. It is rapidly evolving into a new frontier for work, entertainment, and social interaction. Businesses investing in virtual real estate, immersive customer experiences, and digital assets are setting the stage for future success. For individuals, developing skills in VR design, augmented reality (AR) applications, and digital storytelling can open doors to lucrative opportunities.
4. **AI-Driven Personalization**
   AI has reached a point where hyper-personalization is becoming the norm. From healthcare to education to e-commerce, businesses using AI to deliver customized experiences are outperforming their competitors. In 2025, understanding how to harness AI for personalization will be critical for both individuals seeking career advancement and businesses aiming to build deeper customer relationships.

Proactive Strategies for Success

Understanding trends is only the first step; thriving in 2025 requires actionable strategies to capitalize on these shifts. Here are some proven approaches:

- **Diversify Your Skill Set**
  The future belongs to the multi-skilled. Professionals who combine technical knowledge with soft skills like communication, leadership, and emotional intelligence will be in high demand. Consider investing in cross-disciplinary education—such as pairing coding with marketing expertise or combining finance with sustainability knowledge.
- **Invest in High-Growth Industries**
  Identifying and investing in high-growth sectors can accelerate wealth building. From renewable energy stocks to biotech startups and blockchain projects, aligning

your investments with future-oriented industries positions you for exponential growth.

- **Leverage the Gig Economy**
  In 2025, the gig economy will continue to thrive, offering flexibility and financial opportunities. Whether through freelancing, consulting, or creating a side hustle, diversifying income streams mitigates risk and enhances financial stability.

- **Adopt a Resilient Mindset**
  Change often brings challenges, but resilience transforms these obstacles into opportunities. Developing mental toughness, practicing mindfulness, and embracing failure as a stepping stone are essential components of a resilient mindset.

The Role of Networking in a Digital Age

Thriving in 2025 is not a solo endeavor. The most successful individuals understand the importance of building collaborative networks. In the digital age, networking goes beyond attending conferences or exchanging business cards. It involves leveraging social media platforms, joining virtual communities, and forming partnerships that drive mutual growth.

Platforms like LinkedIn and industry-specific forums provide access to thought leaders, potential collaborators, and emerging opportunities. Engaging authentically and providing value to your network will establish you as a trusted authority in your field. Additionally, global connectivity means that opportunities are no longer confined by geography—2025 offers the chance to collaborate with individuals and organizations worldwide.

Looking Ahead: A Future of Endless Possibilities

The year 2025 is a canvas of endless possibilities for those willing to adapt, innovate, and embrace change. By understanding the trends shaping the future and implementing proactive strategies, individuals and businesses can not only survive but thrive in the face of unprecedented transformation.

The key to unlocking success lies in the willingness to reimagine what is possible. The world of 2025 is not static—it is dynamic, interconnected, and brimming with potential. Those who seize the moment and harness the power of change will emerge as leaders, pioneers, and visionaries in this bold new era.

Emerging Trends in Business, Technology, and Personal Development: A Blueprint for Future Prosperity

The future is a dynamic tapestry woven from the threads of innovation, shifting societal norms, and individual aspirations. In a world where rapid change is the only constant, the ability to adapt to emerging trends is not merely an advantage—it is a necessity. As we navigate this era of transformation, understanding the key drivers in business, technology, and personal development becomes critical to unlocking future prosperity. This analysis dives deep into these trends, blending data, insights, and strategies to provide a comprehensive roadmap for success.

Business Trends: Shifting Paradigms in a Globalized Economy

The global business landscape is undergoing a seismic shift, driven by technological advancements, demographic changes, and the pursuit of sustainability. According to a 202 report by the World Economic Forum, over 70% of companies worldwide are now prioritizing digital transformation as a core strategy, with an estimated $2.8 trillion projected to be spent on digital transformation initiatives by 2025. This digital-first approach has catalyzed several key trends:

1. **Rise of Remote Work and Distributed Teams**
   The COVID-19 pandemic permanently altered workplace dynamics, and remote work is here to stay. A 2023 Gartner survey found that 48% of employees in developed economies worked remotely at least par time. By 2030, this number is expected to rise to 60%, as businesses recognize the benefits of reduced overheads and access to a global talent pool.

Remote work has also spurred the growth of distributed teams, where collaboration tools like Slack, Zoom, and Asana have become integral to maintaining productivity. Companies that embrace this trend are not only enhancing operational efficiency but also attracting top talent seeking flexibility.

2. **Sustainability as a Business Imperative**
   Sustainability is no longer a niche concern—it is a central driver of consumer behavior and corporate strategy. Studies indicate that 73% of Gen Z consumers are willing to pay a premium for sustainable products, influencing businesses to prioritize green practices. The renewable energy market alone is projected to grow at a compound annual growth rate (CAGR) of 8.4%, reaching $1.97 trillion by 2030.

Businesses that align with sustainability goals—such as adopting circular economy principles or achieving carbon neutrality—are gaining a competitive edge. Moreover, Environmental, Social, and Governance (ESG) metrics are now critical in attracting investors, with ESG-focused funds accounting for over $2.5 trillion in assets under management as of 2024.

3. **Personalization and Hyper-Segmentation**
   In an age of data abundance, customers expect experiences tailored to their specific needs. The global AI-driven personalization market is projected to reach $2.3 billion by 2025, reflecting a growing emphasis creating customized solutions. Companies that leverage big data and AI to hyper-segment their audience are seeing significant returns, with personalized marketing campaigns yielding 5-8 times higher ROI tha generic approaches.

Technology Trends: The Dawn of Disruptive Innovation

Technology continues to redefine the boundaries of possibility, with advancements in artificial intelligence (AI), quantum computing, and biotechnology leading the charge. These innovations are not just reshaping industries—they are fundamentally altering the way we live, work, and interact.

1. **Artificial Intelligence at the Forefront**
   AI is rapidly transitioning from a niche tool to a mainstream enabler of innovation. By 2025, the global A market is expected to surpass $500 billion, driven by applications ranging from natural language processing (NLP) to autonomous vehicles. AI's ability to analyze vast datasets in real-time is empowerin businesses to make data-driven decisions, enhance customer experiences, and optimize operations.

Generative AI, in particular, has gained traction, with tools like ChatGPT revolutionizing content creation, coding, and customer service. For example, McKinsey estimates that generative AI could add $4.4 trillion annually to the global economy by automating creative and intellectual tasks.

2. **Quantum Computing: A Game-Changer in the Making**
   While still in its infancy, quantum computing promises to solve problems that are currently intractable for classical computers. Industries such as pharmaceuticals, finance, and logistics are poised to benefit from quantum breakthroughs. For instance, quantum algorithms can optimize supply chains, reducing costs by up to 25%. The quantum computing market, valued at $1 billion in 2023, is expected to grow to $10 billion by 2030, signaling its transformative potential.

3. **Biotechnology and HealthTech Innovations**
   The intersection of biology and technology is unlocking new frontiers in healthcare. The global biotechnology market, worth $1.2 trillion in 2024, is projected to grow at a CAGR of 13%, driven by advancements in gene editing, personalized medicine, and biomanufacturing. Tools like CRISPR are enabling scientists to tackle genetic disorders, while wearable devices and AI-powered diagnostics are enhancing preventive care.

Moreover, digital health technologies are bridging gaps in access to care. Telemedicine platforms, for instance, have grown by 60% annually since 2020, offering convenience and reducing healthcare disparities.

Personal Development Trends: Redefining Success in a Fast-Paced World

As external landscapes evolve, so too must our approach to personal growth. Success in the future will not be determined solely by technical skills but also by emotional intelligence, adaptability, and a commitment to continuous learning.

1. **Lifelong Learning as a Non-Negotiable**
   The half-life of skills is shrinking, with many technical skills becoming obsolete within five years. In response, individuals are turning to online platforms for upskilling. Coursera, for example, reported a 30% increase in enrollment in 2023, reflecting the growing demand for accessible education.

Micro-credentials and nanodegrees are also gaining popularity, offering focused, time-efficient ways to acquire new expertise. By 2025, the global online learning market is projected to reach $400 billion, driven by a desire for career resilience in a volatile job market.

2. **The Rise of Mindfulness and Mental Health Awareness**
   In a hyper-connected world, mental well-being is emerging as a cornerstone of personal success. The global mindfulness industry, including apps, retreats, and coaching, is valued at $4 billion and is growing at a steady pace. Tools like Headspace and Calm have brought mindfulness to the masses, helping individuals manage stress and improve focus.

Companies are also prioritizing employee well-being, with over 60% of Fortune 500 firms offering mental health resources as part of their benefits packages. This shift underscores the recognition that a healthy mind is integral to productivity and innovation.

3. **Networking in the Digital Age**
   The importance of networking has only grown in an increasingly virtual world. Platforms like LinkedIn

have become indispensable for career growth, with over 950 million users worldwide. Networking is no longer limited to physical events; virtual communities and online mentorship programs are connecting individuals across borders.

The future belongs to those who can cultivate authentic relationships, provide value to their networks, and leverage these connections for mutual growth.

Interconnected Trends: The Convergence of Business, Technology, and Personal Development

The trends outlined above do not exist in isolation; they are deeply interconnected. For instance, businesses adopting AI and blockchain are not only leveraging technological advancements but also aligning with personal development goals by upskilling their workforce. Similarly, sustainability efforts in business are driving innovation in green technologies while influencing consumer behaviors and lifestyle choices.

This convergence highlights the need for a holistic approach to future prosperity. Thriving in the coming years requires an integrated strategy that encompasses business acumen, technological literacy, and personal growth.

Actionable Insights for Thriving in the Future

1. **Embrace Continuous Learning**
   Commit to acquiring new skills and staying updated on industry trends. Whether through formal education, online courses, or self-directed study, continuous learning is the foundation of adaptability.
2. **Leverage Technology Strategically**
   Stay informed about technological advancements and consider how they can be applied to your personal and professional life. Experiment with AI tools, explore blockchain applications, or delve into the potential of quantum computing.
3. **Prioritize Sustainability**
   Adopt sustainable practices in both your personal and professional spheres. This could involve supporting green businesses, investing in renewable energy, or making eco-friendly lifestyle choices.
4. **Cultivate Emotional Intelligence**
   Develop self-awareness, empathy, and effective communication skills. These traits are invaluable in building relationships and navigating complex challenges.
5. **Build a Resilient Network**
   Expand your network by engaging with like-minded individuals and industry leaders. Focus on building genuine connections that foster collaboration and mutual growth.

The trends shaping our world may seem daunting, but they are also brimming with opportunity. By understanding and embracing these shifts, individuals and businesses can position themselves to not only survive but thrive in an ever-changing landscape. The future is not a distant dream—it is being built today, one decision at a time.

ith the right mindset, tools, and strategies, the path to prosperity is within reach. It is a urney of innovation, resilience, and growth, where those who dare to adapt will 1doubtedly lead the way.

CHAPTER 5: FROM VISION TO REALITY: CREATING AND EXECUTING YOUR MASTER PLAN

The journey from a vision to reality is the bridge between dreaming and doing. Many aspire to greatness, but only a select few achieve it because they lack a clear, actionable master plan. In this chapter, we will delve into the essential steps to transform your aspirations into tangible achievements. It's not just about setting goals; it's about building a strategic roadmap and cultivating the discipline to execute it effectively.

The Power of a Clear Vision

Every great achievement begins with a vision—a compelling picture of what you want to accomplish. A vision is more than a wish or a fleeting idea; it is a vivid, emotionally charged destination that inspires action. When you articulate your vision clearly, it becomes a magnet, pulling you toward your goals and attracting the resources, people, and opportunities you need to succeed.

But vision alone is not enough. Many people stop at this stage, content with imagining what could be. To turn your vision into reality, you must anchor it in specifics. Instead of saying "I want to be financially free," describe what financial freedom looks like for you. Is it owning multiple income-generating assets? Is it the ability to retire early and travel the world? A clear vision is specific, measurable, and deeply personal.

Exercise: Define Your Vision

Take a moment to write down your vision for the next five years. Answer these questions:
- What do you want to achieve?
- Why is this goal important to you?
- How will achieving this change your life?

Be as detailed as possible. Imagine yourself in 2025, living your ideal life. What does your day look like? Who are you with? How do you feel?

SETTING SMART GOALS TO GUIDE YOUR JOURNEY

Once you have a clear vision, the next step is to break it down into actionable goals. This is where the SMART framework comes in:

- **Specific:** Clearly define what you want to achieve.
- **Measurable:** Include metrics to track your progress.
- **Achievable:** Ensure your goals are realistic given your resources.
- **Relevant:** Align your goals with your long-term vision.
- **Time-bound:** Set deadlines to create urgency.

For example, instead of saying, "I want to start a business," a SMART goal would be: "I will launch an online coaching business by June 2025, with a goal of earning $5,000 per month in revenue within the first six months."

Goals are the building blocks of your master plan. They provide structure and direction, ensuring that every step you take moves you closer to your vision.

Crafting Your Master Plan

Your master plan is the blueprint for turning goals into reality. It is a comprehensive, step-by-step strategy that outlines what needs to be done, who will do it, and when it will be completed. Here's how to create one:

Prioritize Your Goals

Not all goals are created equal. Identify the goals that will have the most significant impact on your vision and focus on them first. Use the 80/20 principle, which states that 80% of your results come from 20% of your efforts. Concentrate on the high-impact activities that drive progress.

Break Goals into Milestones

Large goals can feel overwhelming, but breaking them down into smaller milestones makes them more manageable. For example, if your goal is to save $50,000 for a down payment on a house, create monthly savings targets and track your progress.

Allocate Resources

Achieving big goals often requires resources such as time, money, and skills. Assess what you need and create a plan to acquire these resources. This might involve learning new skills, building a network, or securing funding.

Set Deadlines

Deadlines create accountability and momentum. Without them, it's easy to procrastinate. Set realistic deadlines for each milestone and stick to them.

5. Anticipate Challenges

No plan is perfect, and obstacles are inevitable. Anticipate potential challenges and develop contingency plans. If your goal is to grow a side business, for instance, consider how you will balance it with your full-time job or family commitments.

6. Track and Adjust

Your master plan should be a living document. Regularly review your progress, celebrate your wins, and adjust your strategy as needed. Flexibility is key to navigating the inevitable twists and turns of your journey.

The Discipline of Execution

Planning is only half the battle; execution is where the real work begins. Many people falter at this stage, either because they lack discipline or because they get distracted by new ideas and opportunities. Here's how to ensure you stay on track:

1. Create Daily Habits

Success is the result of consistent daily actions. Identify the habits that will move you closer to your goals and incorporate them into your routine. For example, if your goal is to write a book, commit to writing 500 words every morning.

2. Eliminate Distractions

In today's world, distractions are everywhere. Identify the activities that waste your time and energy—whether it's scrolling through social media or binge-watching TV—and eliminate them. Use tools like time-blocking or productivity apps to stay focused.

3. Surround Yourself with Support

Your environment plays a critical role in your success. Surround yourself with people who inspire and challenge you. Join communities of like-minded individuals who share your goals. Their encouragement and accountability can be invaluable.

4. Stay Resilient

Setbacks are inevitable, but resilience is what separates successful people from the rest. When you encounter obstacles, view them as opportunities to learn and grow. Remember, every failure brings you one step closer to success.

Leveraging Technology and Trends in 2025

The world is evolving rapidly, and staying ahead requires leveraging the latest tools and trends. In 2025, technology will play a pivotal role in helping you execute your master plan. Here are some ways to integrate technology into your strategy:

1. Use AI for Productivity

Artificial intelligence can streamline your workflow and save you time. From AI-powered project management tools to virtual assistants, technology can help you stay organized and focused.

2. Embrace Digital Marketing

If your goals involve building a business or personal brand, digital marketing is essential. Invest in tools and platforms that allow you to reach your audience effectively, such as social media advertising and email marketing software.

3. Stay Informed

The pace of change is accelerating, and staying informed is crucial. Subscribe to industry newsletters, attend webinars, and invest in continuous learning to keep your skills and knowledge up to date.

The Power of Reflection and Gratitude

As you work toward your goals, it's important to take time to reflect on your progress and express gratitude. Reflection allows you to assess what's working and what's not, so you can make necessary adjustments. Gratitude, on the other hand, keeps you grounded and motivated.

Exercise: Weekly Reflection

Set aside 30 minutes each week to reflect on your progress. Ask yourself:

- What did I accomplish this week?
- What challenges did I face, and how did I overcome them?
- What can I improve next week?

Write down your thoughts in a journal. This practice will help you stay focused and aligned with your vision.

Creating and executing your master plan is the key to unlocking success. It requires a clear vision, actionable goals, and the discipline to follow through. But the rewards are worth it. By committing to this process, you can turn your dreams into reality and build a life of wealth, freedom, and fulfillment.

Remember, success is not a destination; it's a journey. Embrace the process, stay persistent, and never stop striving for greatness. The future is yours to create—start today.

This draft is designed to resonate with readers looking for actionable strategies to achieve their goals while maintaining the motivational tone typical of Amazon KDP bestsellers. Let me know if you'd like to expand on specific sections!

From Dreams to Achievable Goals: Tools and Strategies for Sustainable Success

Dreams are the seeds of achievement, but too often, they remain abstract aspirations, untethered from reality. The gap between dreaming and doing can feel insurmountable, yet with the right tools and strategies, it is possible to bridge this divide and turn even the loftiest visions into sustainable goals. This chapter delves into the practical methodologies that can transform dreams into actionable, enduring achievements.

THE GAP BETWEEN DREAMING AND DOING: WHY MANY FAIL

A common misconception is that dreaming big is enough. While imagination is the starting point of all progress, dreams without a structure often lead to frustration. People fail to achieve their dreams not because they lack ambition but because they lack clarity, focus, and a system for implementation.

Research suggests that only **8% of people achieve their New Year's resolutions**, a sobering statistic highlighting the gap between intent and action. Common barriers include

1. **Lack of specificity**: Dreams are often vague, lacking clear, actionable objectives.
2. **Overwhelm**: The enormity of a dream can paralyze individuals, leading to inaction.
3. **Absence of accountability**: Without a system of checks, progress falters.
4. **Short-term focus**: Pursuing immediate gratification undermines long-term goals.

The solution lies in transforming dreams into structured goals that are actionable, measurable, and resilient to life's inevitable challenges.

Tool 1: The SMART Framework

The SMART framework is a foundational tool for converting dreams into actionable goals. By providing a structure, it reduces ambiguity and creates a roadmap for success.

Specific

Clarity is power. Replace vague aspirations like "I want to be successful" with clear statements: "I want to increase my annual income to $100,000 by starting an e-commerce business." Specific goals provide direction and eliminate confusion.

Measurable

Metrics matter. Quantify your progress to maintain momentum. If your dream is to "get fit," measure your progress with defined targets like "lose 10 pounds in three months" or "run 5K in under 30 minutes."

Achievable

Dream big, but stay grounded. Goals must stretch your abilities without being impossible. Assess your resources, skills, and constraints. A goal of becoming a world-renowned chef is admirable, but it should start with enrolling in culinary school.

Relevant

Align goals with your core values and long-term vision. If your dream is financial independence, prioritize goals like building passive income streams over short-term material purchases.

Time-bound

Deadlines create urgency and prevent procrastination. Break long-term dreams into smaller, time-specific milestones. For instance, "Launch my business by June 2025" creates a sense of urgency and commitment.

Applying the SMART Framework

Let's apply SMART principles to a common dream: publishing a book.

1. **Specific**: "I will write and self-publish a 60,000-word novel."
2. **Measurable**: "I will write 2,000 words per week and complete the first draft in six months."
3. **Achievable**: Ensure time and resources are available, such as dedicating two hours daily to writing.
4. **Relevant**: Align the project with personal and professional aspirations, such as becoming a published author.
5. **Time-bound**: Set clear deadlines for each stage: drafting, editing, and publishing.

Tool 2: Vision Boards and Visualization

Visualization is a powerful psychological tool that bridges dreams and goals. Athletes, entrepreneurs, and innovators alike harness this technique to maintain focus and motivation.

Vision Boards

A vision board is a visual representation of your dreams. It serves as a constant reminder of your goals and keeps you emotionally connected to your aspirations. To create one:

- Collect images, quotes, and symbols that represent your goals.
- Arrange them on a board in a place you see daily.
- Regularly update it to reflect evolving ambitions.

The Science Behind Visualization

Neuroscience confirms that visualization activates the brain's **reticular activating system (RAS)**, which filters relevant information and primes the mind for success. By vividly imagining your success, you train your brain to identify opportunities and take actions that align with your goals.

Guided Visualization Exercise

1. Close your eyes and imagine yourself achieving your dream in vivid detail.
2. Engage all senses: What do you see, hear, feel, and even smell?
3. Repeat this practice daily to solidify your mental connection to the goal.

STRATEGY 1: REVERSE ENGINEERING YOUR DREAM

Reverse engineering is a strategy that starts with the end goal and works backward to define the necessary steps. It's particularly effective for complex, long-term dreams.

Steps to Reverse Engineer Your Dream

1. **Define the Endpoint**: Clearly articulate what success looks like.
2. **Identify Milestones**: Break the goal into manageable phases.
3. **List Necessary Actions**: Determine the tasks required for each phase.
4. **Set Timelines**: Assign deadlines to each task and milestone.

Example: Launching a Tech Startup

- **Endpoint**: A fully operational startup generating $500,000 in revenue annually.
- **Milestone 1**: Develop a product prototype.
- **Milestone 2**: Secure seed funding.
- **Milestone 3**: Launch the product to market.
- **Milestone 4**: Scale operations.

Each milestone is further broken into actionable tasks, such as conducting market research, building a development team, and creating a marketing strategy.

Strategy 2: Building Systems, Not Just Goals

While goals provide direction, systems create sustainable progress. A goal is a destination; a system is the daily practice that gets you there.

Why Systems Matter

Goals can feel daunting, but systems focus on the process. Instead of fixating on "losing 20 pounds," create a system of daily healthy habits: exercising for 30 minutes, preparing nutritious meals, and tracking calories.

Designing Effective Systems

1. **Identify Keystone Habits**: Keystone habits are small changes that trigger positive ripple effects. For example, regular exercise improves energy levels, productivity, and self-discipline.
2. **Automate Repetitive Tasks**: Use tools and technology to streamline actions, such as setting automatic savings transfers or using productivity apps.
3. **Evaluate Regularly**: Periodically review your systems to ensure they align with your goals and adapt as needed.

Tool 3: Accountability Mechanisms

Accountability is a cornerstone of goal achievement. Studies show that people are **65% more likely to reach their goals when they share them with a partner** and **95% more likely when they commit to regular accountability check-ins.**

Forms of Accountability

1. **Accountability Partners**: Share your goals with a trusted friend or mentor who can provide encouragement and honest feedback.
2. **Goal-Setting Groups**: Join or form a community of like-minded individuals with similar aspirations.
3. **Public Declarations**: Announcing your goals publicly adds a layer of pressure and motivation.

Tracking Progress

Regular tracking ensures you stay on course. Use journals, apps, or spreadsheets to document milestones, challenges, and adjustments. Reflecting on your progress reinforces commitment and highlights areas for improvement.

Strategy 3: Embracing Flexibility

Rigid plans often crumble under the weight of unforeseen challenges. Flexibility ensures resilience. While your vision remains constant, your strategies and timelines should adapt to changing circumstances.

The Pivot Mindset

Adopting a pivot mindset allows you to shift approaches without abandoning the dream. For instance, if one business strategy fails, analyze the failure, recalibrate, and try another approach.

Learning from Setbacks

Setbacks are not failures; they are feedback. Analyze what went wrong, extract lessons, and apply them to future efforts. Embrace a growth mindset that views challenges as opportunities for improvement.

STRATEGY 4: THE ROLE OF REWARDS AND CELEBRATIONS

Celebrating progress fuels motivation. Each milestone achieved is a step closer to the dream, and recognizing these moments reinforces positive behavior.

Designing a Reward System

1. **Micro-Rewards**: Celebrate small wins, such as completing a week of consistent work. Treat yourself to something enjoyable, like a favorite meal or a relaxing activity.
2. **Macro-Rewards**: For significant milestones, plan larger rewards, such as a weekend getaway or a new purchase.

The Path to Sustainability

Sustainability ensures that your achievements are not fleeting. It's not enough to reach a goal; you must build systems that maintain success. For instance, if your dream is to achieve financial independence, focus on creating multiple income streams that endure economic fluctuations.

Key Pillars of Sustainability

1. **Consistency**: Develop habits that integrate your goals into your daily life.
2. **Adaptability**: Remain open to innovation and continuous improvement.
3. **Legacy Thinking**: Aim to build something that lasts beyond immediate gratification.

By combining the right tools, strategies, and mindset, you can transform your dreams into actionable, sustainable goals. Success is not a matter of luck or talent—it's the result of deliberate planning and persistent effort. The journey may be challenging, but with a clear vision, robust systems, and unwavering commitment, the destination is within reach.

Tool/Strategy	Description	Key Components	Example Application
SMART Framework	A goal-setting framework to provide clarity, focus, and measurability to your objectives.	Specific, Measurable, Achievable, Relevant, Time-bound.	"Write and self-publish a 60,000-word book by December 2025, drafting 2,000 words per week."
Vision Boards and Visualization	Visual and mental techniques to reinforce emotional connection to goals and prime the brain for success.	Vision boards with images and quotes; guided daily visualization exercises.	Creating a vision board with images of financial independence and visualizing its impact.
Reverse Engineering	A planning method starting with the end goal and mapping backward to actionable steps.	Define endpoint, set milestones, list required actions, assign timelines.	Launching a tech startup: Prototype > Funding > Launch > Scale operations.
Building Systems	Establishing sustainable habits and routines that focus on daily progress rather than distant goals.	Keystone habits, automation, regular evaluations.	Exercising daily and tracking meals to achieve long-term fitness goals.
Accountability Mechanisms	Creating systems to track progress and maintain motivation through external or internal accountability.	Accountability partners, goal-setting groups, public declarations.	Sharing weekly progress with a mentor or a support group.
Flexibility	Adapting strategies and timelines while keeping the vision intact.	Pivot mindset, learning from setbacks, embracing growth.	Adjusting a marketing strategy after analyzing campaign failures.
Rewards and Celebrations	Motivational tools to acknowledge progress and maintain enthusiasm.	Micro-rewards for small wins, macro-rewards for significant milestones.	Rewarding oneself with a favorite activity after meeting a quarterly goal.
Sustainability Practices	Ensuring achievements are maintained long-term by creating resilient systems and focusing on legacy.	Consistency, adaptability, legacy thinking.	Building passive income streams to sustain financial independence.

APPENDICES

I n this section, you'll find a curated toolkit, real-life case studies, and practical templates designed to help you deepen your understanding of the concepts discussed throughout the book and apply them to your life with precision and purpose.

RESOURCE TOOLKIT: BOOKS, TOOLS, AND COURSES TO ACCELERATE YOUR SUCCESS

The following resources have been carefully selected to provide you with further insights and actionable strategies for achieving your dreams and turning them into sustainable goals.

Books

1. **"Atomic Habits" by James Clear**
   - Focus: Building effective habits and breaking bad ones.
   - Why Read: Clear offers a practical framework for making small changes that lead to significant transformations.
2. **"The 7 Habits of Highly Effective People" by Stephen R. Covey**
   - Focus: Principles of personal and professional effectiveness.
   - Why Read: A timeless classic on aligning actions with values and priorities.
3. **"Deep Work" by Cal Newport**
   - Focus: The ability to focus without distraction in a world filled with noise.
   - Why Read: Learn how to produce high-quality work and achieve extraordinary results in less time.
4. **"Your Best Year Ever" by Michael Hyatt**
   - Focus: Setting and achieving meaningful goals.
   - Why Read: A step-by-step guide to designing a life you love through intentional goal-setting.
5. **"Think and Grow Rich" by Napoleon Hill**
   - Focus: Mindset, persistence, and strategies for wealth-building.
   - Why Read: Discover timeless principles for personal success and financial freedom.

Tools

1. **Trello or Asana**
   - Purpose: Project management and task tracking.
   - Why Use: Organize your goals into actionable tasks and track your progress effortlessly.
2. **Notion**
   - Purpose: All-in-one workspace for notes, tasks, and project tracking.
   - Why Use: Customize templates to plan your goals, track milestones, and stay on top of deadlines.
3. **Habitica**
   - Purpose: Habit tracking through gamification.
   - Why Use: Make forming habits fun by earning rewards for completing tasks.
4. **Evernote**
   - Purpose: Note-taking and organization.
   - Why Use: Capture ideas, brainstorm, and organize thoughts in one place.
5. **Google Calendar**
   - Purpose: Scheduling and time management.
   - Why Use: Plan your days, weeks, and months effectively, ensuring every task is accounted for.

Courses
1. **"Learning How to Learn" by Dr. Barbara Oakley (Coursera)**
    - Focus: Strategies to improve learning efficiency.
    - Why Take: Master the science of learning and apply it to any goal.
2. **"Time Management Mastery" by Brian Tracy (Udemy)**
    - Focus: Effective time management techniques.
    - Why Take: Learn how to prioritize tasks and manage your day like a pro.
3. **"Goal Setting & Personal Productivity" by Skillshare**
    - Focus: Defining and achieving goals.
    - Why Take: Practical tips and exercises to sharpen your focus and discipline.
4. **"Masterclass with Robin Arzón: Mental Strength and Discipline"**
    - Focus: Building resilience and pushing boundaries.
    - Why Take: Learn how to cultivate mental toughness from one of the world's leading fitness coaches.
5. **"Financial Independence and Early Retirement" by ChooseFI (Online Community)**
    - Focus: Creating financial freedom.
    - Why Take: Gain insights from real-life stories and actionable advice on managing money effectively.

CASE STUDIES: REAL STORIES OF PEOPLE WHO TRANSFORMED THEIR LIVES

Real-life examples bring concepts to life, showing how ordinary people used extraordinary principles to achieve success.

Case Study 1: Sarah's Journey to Entrepreneurship

- **Dream**: Sarah wanted to leave her corporate job to start her own handmade jewelry business.
- **Strategy Applied**: Sarah used the SMART framework to break her dream into clear, actionable steps. She began by setting a specific goal: "Launch an online jewelry store with at least 20 designs by December 2024."
- **Outcome**: Sarah achieved her goal by building a daily habit of dedicating two hours after work to her craft and leveraging tools like Shopify to manage her online store. Within a year, she transitioned to full-time entrepreneurship.

Case Study 2: David's Fitness Transformation

- **Dream**: David aimed to lose weight and run a marathon.
- **Strategy Applied**: David created a system rather than focusing solely on the end goal. He committed to exercising 30 minutes daily, tracking his meals, and joining a local running group for accountability.
- **Outcome**: Over 18 months, David lost 50 pounds and completed his first marathon. He credits his success to small, consistent actions rather than overwhelming himself with unrealistic goals.

Case Study 3: Priya's Academic Achievement

- **Dream**: Priya aspired to earn a scholarship to study abroad.
- **Strategy Applied**: Priya reverse-engineered her goal. She identified the requirements, such as test scores, recommendation letters, and essays, and worked backward to create a detailed timeline. Priya used visualization techniques to stay motivated and frequently updated her vision board with images of her dream university.
- **Outcome**: Priya secured a full scholarship to her desired institution and is now pursuing her master's degree.

Case Study 4: Alex's Financial Freedom Plan

- **Dream**: Alex wanted to achieve financial independence by age 40.
- **Strategy Applied**: Alex adopted a dual approach of goal-setting and systems. He set clear financial milestones, automated his savings, and educated himself on passive income strategies through books and courses.
- **Outcome**: By his 39th birthday, Alex had built a diversified portfolio of investments that provided him with enough income to retire early and pursue his passion for teaching.

GOAL-SETTING TEMPLATES AND WORKSHEETS

Practical tools make it easier to translate dreams into action. Below are templates and worksheets to guide your journey.

1. Goal-Setting Template

Objective: Break down your goals using the SMART framework.

Goal	Details
Specific	Clearly define your goal. Example: "Write a 60,000-word novel by December 2025."
Measurable	Identify how to track progress. Example: "Write 2,000 words weekly."
Achievable	Assess feasibility. Example: "Dedicate two hours daily to writing."
Relevant	Align with your values. Example: "Publishing aligns with my career as an aspiring author."
Time-bound	Set deadlines. Example: "First draft by June 2025, final edits by November 2025."

2. Weekly Progress Tracker

Objective: Monitor and reflect on your weekly progress.

Week	Goal	Actions Taken	Challenges Faced	Adjustments Needed
Week 1	Write 2,000 words	Wrote daily, but missed Sunday	Time management issues	Schedule writing earlier in the day
Week 2	Complete market research	Surveyed 50 potential customers	Difficulty reaching target group	Use social media to expand outreach

3. Daily Habit Tracker

Objective: Track habits that align with your goals.

Date	Habit	Completed?	Notes
Jan 1	Exercise 30 minutes	✓	Felt energized afterward
Jan 2	Read 10 pages of a book	✗	Got busy; prioritize earlier in the day
Jan 3	Meditate for 10 minutes	✓	Helped me focus on tasks throughout the day

4. Vision Board Checklist

Objective: Build an effective vision board.

Step	Completed?
Identify core dreams/goals	✓
Gather inspiring images/quotes	✓
Arrange them on a board	✓
Place board in a visible spot	✓
Update regularly	☐

5. Milestone Planner

Objective: Break down long-term goals into actionable milestones.

Milestone	Deadline	Action Steps
Launch e-commerce store	June 2025	Register domain, design website, upload product catalog, run ads
Write a book	December 2025	Create outline, write chapters, edit, format, and self-publish

These appendices are designed to equip you with both inspiration and practical tools. By leveraging these resources, real-life stories, and templates, you can bridge the gap between dreaming and doing—and make extraordinary success your reality.

END